KU-372-864

Contents WITHDRAWN

1. What is time management?

Time management is considered a very important business skill. It is essentially about spending the hours and minutes in the day as effectively as possible.

There are very few occupations where people don't have a choice about how they organise their work. An exception might be trainee soldiers in boot camp, where the sergeant major controls every minute – but this is far from normal. Even in appointment-based roles – for instance, doctors, hairdressers or sales representatives – people need to set aside time for preparation and administrative tasks. Most of us have some self-determination – even at school or college, with fixed timetables and deadlines you can choose how to use study periods or lunch breaks, when to do homework and how to organise revision for exams.

Like many areas of business life good time management is a combination of common sense, some basic techniques and experience over time to develop good working habits.

Most people think there are more things they need to do, or would like to do, than they have time for in their life. This happens a lot at work, and often results in working overtime, frustration and stress and feelings of guilt or panic if deadlines aren't met. Good time management won't remove the inevitable pressures and conflicts that arise in most jobs. But it should help make the working day more satisfying and calm.

Some questions to ask yourself are:

❑ Am I using my time to address the most important things I have to do?

1

❑ What things happen to stop me working well?

❑ Do I start each day with a clear idea of what I want to achieve?

❑ Do colleagues (and friends) see me as competent or disorganised?

The main things you need to address to manage your time well are:

1. Be clear about the objectives and priorities of your role.

2. Plan your time based on a thorough assessment of the work you need to do, and take into account the interruptions that inevitably occur.

3. Keep a diary and action list so they work for you.

4. Get organised – turn your workstation into a tool bench rather than a half-finished jigsaw puzzle.

5. Watch out for the gremlin time wasters – the 'minute burglars' – and guard against them.

6. Communicate effectively with the people around you.

Why do I need to know about time management?

Your company is paying a salary for your time. So each unit of time costs money. You have a responsibility to spend your employer's money wisely. Just based on annual salary, this table shows the cost of time:

Annual salary	1 day	1 hour	10 minutes
£8,000	£38.94	£5.56	£0.93
£10,000	£48.67	£6.95	£1.16
£15,000	£73.01	£10.43	£1.74
£18,000	£87.61	£12.52	£2.09
£20,000	£97.35	£13.91	£2.32
£25,000	£121.68	£17.38	£2.90
£30,000	£146.02	£20.86	£3.48

So if you're earning £15,000 the ten minutes it takes you to get a cup of coffee is £1.74 of your time. Of course, most employers don't begrudge the coffee break, or count your time in that way. But if that and all the other wasted ten minutes mean you are not coping with your job, you're either seriously overworked or you need to examine your time management.

Once time has been used it can't be replaced. The 30 minutes you spend watching a really bad television programme, for instance, will never happen again (but hopefully the television programme won't either!) What else could you have done with that half-hour that would have been an achievement rather than a loss?

Knowing how to plan your work, and tackle it effectively has a lot of benefits. You will increase your achievements and spend less effort making up for lost time. You will be able to set aside time for thinking, and important tasks, and so produce better results – which will make the day much more rewarding and stress-free. It will also be obvious to people around you that you are competent at your work – so chances of working on interesting projects or getting promotion are more likely to come your way.

How can I tell if I need to improve my time management?

Here is a quick checklist – do any of these things apply to you now?

- ❏ Do you often need to work overtime or at weekends?
- ❏ Are deadlines missed and projects delayed?
- ❏ Does everything seem equally urgent – are there no priorities?
- ❏ Is the day about 'fire-fighting' – dealing with crises rather than structured for ongoing work?
- ❏ Do you have trouble finding the right information to deal with a project?
- ❏ Do meetings get cancelled at the last minute?

❑ Can you say no to requests – or does the work just pile up?

❑ Do you feel stressed and out of control?

❑ Do your friends or relations complain that you never have time for them?

Is there any special training or tools?

Most business training companies run time management courses because the ability to manage conflicting pressures is so important at work. There is the TimeManagement™ system, electronic diaries, project planning software and a host of other products available.

Good time management is about putting the techniques and tools into practice and establishing working patterns or habits that are effective. For instance, if you spend an hour a day synchronising your personal diary, the computer system at work, and a desk diary, that's 33 working days a year. No wonder so many people work unpaid overtime!

2. How do I get started on good time management habits?

Even if you don't read any further in this book do this simple exercise –
it will make you think more clearly about your own time management.
Write down the following for your working day, or better yet – your life:

1. What are my goals and priorities?

2. What is on my 'to do' list?

3. What things waste my time?

It's true for everyone that quite a bit on the 'to do' list and all of the time
wasters block most of the good things you can do to reach your goals
and objectives.

The first step to better time management – make a list

A very simple start to good practice is to write a list every evening
before you go home of things you need to do – the big and the little,
including tasks that can be achieved in one day and ongoing projects.

If you check and update this daily, you will always know the work in
hand and have an idea of each day's workload. Deadlines won't creep
up on you suddenly, and you'll know the things you have achieved as
you tick them off the list. (Structuring your list well is looked at on pages
16–19.)

Once you are in the habit of keeping tabs on your workload with a simple action list, you can start to control your work by reviewing what needs to be done and prioritising.

Review your action list and set priorities

If a new task, idea or job comes up, review how important it is given your own priorities:

❑ If it is simple do it immediately if you possibly can – or give it to someone else to do.

❑ Don't add it to the action list, put it in a pile to deal with or think about later.

❑ If it's not that important – throw it away.

❑ If it's very important, spend 10 minutes thinking time reviewing options and courses of action. Your brain will probably do that anyway – so give it the space.

Top time tip – tick off a task quick

Amy Bell is a personnel manager in a large food manufacturer. She has a lot of administrative tasks each day. Her top tip is: 'The first thing I do every morning is read my list of things to do. I choose a task I can do immediately, and I complete it. You start the day in a much more positive frame of mind knowing you have already achieved something, and ticked it off the list.'

How do I understand my goals and priorities?

If you are very lucky your employer or manager will spend a lot of time establishing work objectives with you, and provide counselling and training so you can meet them.

In the adult working world the truth is that you will more often have to take this responsibility on yourself. This is a very powerful thing to do – so don't feel aggrieved if the personal counselling isn't on tap.

Evaluate your own goals

To understand what your priorities should be, evaluate your goals, define the objectives to reach them and the steps or actions needed.

Some long-term goals might be to get a promotion, or develop marketing skills. In order to get a promotion you might need to:

❑ Improve your performance in key areas of your job.

❑ Take on extra responsibilities.

❑ Know how to write business proposals and reports.

❑ Find out about the opportunities in your company, and get career advice.

❑ Learn how to manage other people.

So, you have identified a broad goal, now you need to work on the specific objectives to achieve the goal, and the tasks you need to undertake for each objective.

Objectives should be S M A R T:

> **S**pecific
> **M**easurable
> **A**chievable
> **R**ealistic
> **T**imed

For instance, you may have a goal of living in a nicer house. A specific objective might be to have saved £5000 for a deposit in 12 months' time. That is specific and measurable – and timed – but is it achievable and realistic?

What are the tasks you need to undertake to achieve it? What are the actions you can take?

❑ Set up a high-interest savings account.

❑ Arrange a direct debit from your current account to the savings account.

❑ Get an evening or weekend job to supplement your income.

❑ Sell things you don't use any more – the electric guitar or stamp collection.

❑ Find out how to spend less on travel – would a season ticket loan reduce your train fares overall?

Once you have thought about all the options and alternatives you decide which actions should be your priorities, how much time they will take and set some timescales and targets. You won't be able to do everything tomorrow, but if you have a 'strategic plan' for achieving the objective, the probability that you will get there is much, much greater.

Of course, most people have more than one goal in life – so there are lots of objectives to aim for, and in a work context this is particularly true. Time management is really about balancing them all effectively.

The first step is to write them all down – get a sheet of paper and capture your goals, then the objectives to achieve them. Keep this in your diary and refer to it often.

If you take some time to think about all your goals, establish objectives and plan out the tasks to achieve them, you will very quickly identify the important things to do on a daily basis. On pages 15–16 there is a further example about planning a project.

Each task you undertake should work towards your objectives. If it doesn't, why are you spending the time on it?

Let's take an example: Frank Speaker works in customer support for a computer company. Every week he has to:

❑ Handle telephone calls from users who have problems

❑ Prepare documentation

❑ Set up and run training courses for clients

❑ Learn about new software and technology

❑ Train new staff

❑ Attend weekly team meetings

❑ Complete a timesheet showing how he has spent his time.

Frank has three objectives:

1. Train users

2. Support users

3. Help the department run efficiently.

Frank often works late to prepare documentation and read papers that accumulate during the day. He thinks that several things he has to do are a waste of time – which he tells his supervisor frequently! But how does he actually spend his day?

How do I evaluate my day and find the time wasters?

There are some work roles where it is necessary to complete timesheets – not always because managers are control freaks, but because clients are charged by time for work. This is true for jobs at all levels, like lawyers, creative teams in advertising agencies, mechanics, and beauty consultants.

In order to save time, you need to find out how you spend it – so keeping a timesheet for a few days is a very good way of identifying time wasters. It will also make you more conscious of what you are doing.

Note down the time, the action, what sort of work it is, whether it was planned or caused by an interruption. At the end of the day, tally up the time spent on each type of work. As an example, on the next page is Frank's timesheet.

Start time	Activity	Category	Planned	Mins
09:00	Coffee, read mail, chat	General		15
09:15	Get files out to work on report about course participants	Thinking/writing	P	15
09:30	Telephone call from angry customer, with big problem about a course run last week	Telephone		5
09:35	Discuss phone call with colleagues	Meeting		10
09:45	Discuss phone call with manager	Meeting		10
09:55	Write email about problem to manager so another department can call customer back	Correspond-ence		15
10:10	Get coffee	General		5
10:15	Go to the toilet	General		5
10:20	Check and read email	General		10
10:30	Go to staff meeting	General	P	10
10:40	Staff meeting starts – late	General		25
11:05	Get coffee	General		5
11:10	Listen to telephone messages and call customer back	Telephone		15
11:25	Work on report – start reading file again	Thinking/writing		20
11:45	Telephone call from friend about seeing a film	Telephone		10
11:55	Check web sites for film reviews	General		5
12:00	Lunch time			

Half the day has gone and only 35 minutes has been spent writing an important report. Can you spot the time wasters?

Typical time wasters

In every company or job there will be thousands of lurking 'minute burglars'. These are some of the obvious examples:

❏ The dead time between meetings or appointments– when there is not enough time to start a big task, as you wait for a meeting to start or client to arrive.

❏ Not being able to find documents or information needed to work on.

❏ Unnecessary travel – spending time visiting a client or attending one meeting rather than planning a series of visits in a day.

❏ Social chats and corridor meetings with colleagues. Work stops for coffee.

❏ Not knowing how to use equipment or computer software properly – so spending time fiddling or getting frustrated.

❏ Unnecessary or overlong meetings.

❏ Telephone calls that you shouldn't deal with.

❏ Telephone conversations that go on for too long.

❏ Spending too long on simple or unimportant tasks that should be done quickly.

❏ Interruptions from drop-in visitors – colleagues who want advice, managers who want to find something out, building maintenance checking on the air-conditioning or power supply.

❏ Emergencies and crises creating general panic.

❏ Lack of planning and priority setting, so time is spent doing work which isn't really necessary.

You can't avoid all of these, but you can learn how to deal with them – to use dead time to do something positive, to keep interruptions short, and to schedule your workload to the time available.

Top time tip – don't be a perfectionist when you don't have to

Emma Kulate works in a marketing company where she often runs presentations for clients. She likes the job, which is about getting the details right, as she's a natural perfectionist. But it did have its downside.

'Doing presentations everything has to be just right. You have to make sure the room is set up with enough chairs, all the equipment is functioning, you have the right number of handouts, and you have to look your best all the time – the list goes on. Unfortunately I started to do everything the way I do a presentation – making sure everything is perfect, always. That's pretty stressful.

'Then I realised that although I like to do my job well, I don't have to be a perfectionist all the time. I can cut corners and do things "adequately" when it's not so important. I don't have to spellcheck memos I write for myself, or proofread all my assistant's letters, or spend hours designing a report like it's a marketing leaflet. Now I don't get so worked up about things, I recognise where the effort really matters, and it makes me better at focusing on the client's needs rather than my own attention to detail.'

How do I make my workspace more efficient?

While some people think that a jumbled workspace with papers piled high is the sign of a busy and hardworking person, in fact untidiness does waste time. Spending 20 seconds filing a document when you've finished with it saves 20 minutes looking for it when you need it next. Knowing where everything you need is instantly saves those minutes spent searching through a drawer, pile of papers, or shelf-load of files and books. Good management of paper and files is discussed on pages 23–25.

In a typical office your desk could have on its surface:

❑ a telephone

❑ a notepad

- ❏ a container with pens and pencils
- ❏ a computer screen and keyboard if you have one (put the tower below decks if possible)
- ❏ the current papers or materials you are working on
- ❏ a coffee cup
- ❏ a single in-tray
- ❏ your diary and work planner.

All the extras – ruler, hole-puncher, tape, glue, scissors, staples, post-it notes, dictionary, packed lunch, mobile phone and personal organiser – should be stored safely in a desk drawer.

The fluffy toy, misty picture of your partner in the large gold frame, Tamagotchi, Olympics baseball cap, souvenir paperweight shell from the beach holiday in Corfu, half-completed tapestry, incense burner, voodoo doll of your ex-partner, latest copy of *Hello!* magazine and ankle exercise weights should all be left at home. Your workstation is for work, not diversion.

Work in progress files should be near to hand – eg in a desk drawer or filing cabinet. Your in-tray is unlikely to be effective if it is a towering multistorey construction.

How do I use my diary?

Diaries are central to good time management. At the minimum you should record in one place the fixed events – meetings and travel time, holidays and deadlines for work projects – and refer to it regularly.

If you think of a diary as a time calendar and planner it becomes a much more powerful tool. It's helpful to have enough space to write notes and reminders for each day, or to keep your action list.

For instance, if you have to do a stock check every Tuesday, on Mondays make a note to ensure you have all the latest stocklists and any special requests made that week. Book enough time in your diary on Tuesday – if you know it takes an hour, book an hour, there's no point saving a 45-minute slot. (The job will take twice as long if you don't finish it and have to pick it up again later, or you cut corners to save time when you should be taking extra care with figures.)

You can also record reminders to call people if you have said you will contact them again, and note deadlines for work projects or tasks on the day they are due.

In planning your work:

❑ Set regular times during the day to deal with any correspondence, email and phone calls.

❑ Schedule active tasks first but build in time to allow for interruptions, and reactive tasks.

❑ Avoid lots of short periods – try for continuous stretches and work somewhere you won't be interrupted if necessary.

❑ Work on things that need maximum brain power when you are at your best.

❑ Avoid back-to-back meetings and appointments.

❑ Try to complete one task before starting the next.

❑ Aim to achieve something each day.

❑ Review your diary daily to allow for changing priorities.

❑ If you have a big project to complete then assign blocks of free time in your diary to concentrate on it.

Top time tip – tick to your body clock

As the owner and manager of a garden centre, Carl Tevait has a wide variety of work to do, from basic office administration to accounting and stock control. His top tip is: 'It's important to work out your own body clock. If you're most active in the morning, do the complicated "thinking" tasks before 12, such as writing reports, doing the accounts. If your body and your brain shut down for an hour after lunch, use that time to do less complicated administrative things like filing, photocopying and answering requests for information.'

What is a time planner and when would I use it?

Time planners are more sophisticated systems, which combine diaries with action lists, and they are incredibly useful if your job involves projects with many stages and actions, which you need to set time for.

At a macro level you have a year plan – with the major goals to be achieved. This can be broken down into months, with key objectives. In each month there are a set of actions to complete, which can then be assigned to weeks or days – and this becomes your action list.

Let's take an example. Your manager has given you the task of reviewing the vending machines in your office and suggesting ways of saving money. You have three months to complete the report. What do you need to do?

1. Find out about the existing machines, how much they cost, who provides them and what they are for.
2. Find out about problems in using them.
3. Research alternatives and the costs involved.
4. Compare options, and check company policy on suppliers, health and safety and office layout.
5. Draft a report of your findings and conclusions.
6. Check the report, ask your manager to review it and fill in missing information.
7. Circulate the report.
8. Present the main points to your manager.

So you divide the work down over time:

Month 1	Month 2	Month 3
● Research existing machines ● Ask users	● Research other suppliers & compare ● Draft report & check	● Extra research ● Finish report ● Presentation

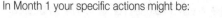

In Month 1 your specific actions might be:

- ❑ Meet with the building services manager for a briefing.
- ❑ Read the supplier contracts from the vending machine operators.
- ❑ Get the management accountant to provide financial reports and summarise them.
- ❑ Send a questionnaire to staff and analyse the response.

So on Day 1 you might spend one hour on the project and:

- ❑ Set an appointment with the building services manager.
- ❑ Set an appointment with the management accountant.
- ❑ Look round the building and take notes to ask questions.

Suddenly a big project becomes a series of do-able actions that can fit alongside all the other work you need to do. Next week and next month can be broken down in the same way, if you spend time at the beginning of each week and month planning your work.

Alternatively you could do nothing for two and a half months and then panic and work late, but the results won't be anywhere near as good.

How do I keep an action list?

Everyone has an action list, even if it's only in their head, so you already understand the rudiments.

Must do soon
Go shopping for food for dinner
Send granny a birthday card
Renew bus pass
Call friends and arrange a drink
Sort out holiday photos
Pay phone bill
Get a tattoo (tasteful only)
Feed the cat
Fill in application form for new job

Some actions are urgent, some are important, some are fun, some are completely unnecessary and some are frankly boring.

Whether you are at work or organising your personal life there are several time management tricks you can use:

❏ Establish habits to deal with the routine tasks quickly so you don't need to write them down (eg feed the cat, and shop for food).

❏ Record all your actions in one place (multiple post-it notes and reminders on the pinboard will get overlooked).

❏ Sort out whether you should be doing the action – or is it someone else's job?

❏ Prioritise. Not all actions have equal importance and benefits. Refer back to your list of goals and objectives and then decide which box the task fits in. You can bin the ones that aren't important or urgent immediately!

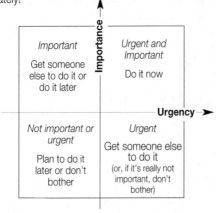

So the most valuable thing to do is evaluate the importance of all those things hanging over your head. Some will be important and urgent. Others might be nice ideas – so take them away from your action list and store them in an ideas file – then make an action to look at the file regularly.

The simplest list of tasks could be constructed like this. You will add more items to the list, and complete others not on the list.

Action	Details		Urgency (A B C)	Deadline
1.				
2.				
3.				
4.				

An alternative way of organising an action list is by project area. Construct a table that covers the main areas of your job or the people you deal with, and write down the actions needed, and deadline dates. If you are working on several distinct projects this method is more useful than a general action list.

	Date due
Monthly report Get statistics Ask about credit to customer	
Boss Review press articles	
New training course Review feedback forms Telephone top five customers Ask accounts for booking figures	
Administration Assistant Check course material is ready Check room arrangements for meeting	

Whichever action list format you choose:

❑ Don't spend time rewriting it every day – plan on revising it once a week, so leave space to add new items, and cross off the ones you have completed.

❑ Use colour or symbols to highlight the really urgent tasks.

❑ Make a note of deadlines in your diary.

❑ Write clearly.

Each day you should look at the list and your diary and evaluate the urgent and important tasks. Set yourself an achievable action list for the day. For instance – you won't be able to edit and summarise a 50-page report if you are in an all-day training course.

Top time tip – differentiate 'urgent' and 'important'

Annie de Braek is a solicitor in a city law firm. She deals with a lot of big-name clients and is constantly having to prioritise a heavy workload. She explains how essential it is that she makes the distinction between 'important' and urgent'.

'Every single job I have I consider carefully. If, for instance, on Monday morning I have a contract between two existing clients to get out by Friday, that's important. If I also have to write a proposal letter to pitch for new business, and it's got to be in by the end of the day, that's important too, but it's also urgent. If I don't do it, I'll have missed the deadline and the opportunity.'

---

3. How can I use time better during the day?

If you examine all the routine tasks you do, there will probably be some that are taking much longer than is strictly necessary – telephone calls, email, or mountains of paper. Use some of the simple techniques for saving time on these standard tasks outlined in the follow sections, and get into the habit of good practice.

How do I save time when making telephone calls?

The key to making your telephone calls as brief and effective as possible is preparation.

❑ Decide whom you should contact, and think of alternatives. If you can't get through can you contact someone else or send an email?

❑ Choose a good time of day to call – are they likely to be at their desk first thing in the morning or are afternoons better?

❑ Write out the telephone number, name of the person and make notes on what you want to say, or find out – with the important facts and dates written down.

❑ Be prepared to leave a message if your reach a secretary or voicemail, which explains concisely why you are calling.

❑ Keep any additional paperwork handy.

❑ Have a paper and pen ready.

❑ Relax by breathing deeply (but not loudly at the person on the other end of the line – you could be arrested).

❑ Visualise the person you will be speaking to.

❑ Smile and dial. (The smile will show in your tone of voice and will help you to speak clearly.)

❑ Keep a timer or clock near your phone to keep the calls short.

❑ Keep the conversation focused. It is polite to exchange pleasantries – don't let the conversation drift to other subjects. A play-by-play review of last night's football game is not appropriate.

If you have a lot of telephone calls to make the most efficient way of handling them is to make them all during one or two specific times during the day.

Top time tip – don't phone when others are 'out to lunch'

Colin Hoftan works in a company that compiles and designs brochures and annual reports for other organisations. He has to check a lot of information by phone, and has worked out when are the best times: 'I try never to call anyone for important information before lunch on Mondays or after lunch on Fridays. People are either very busy, or not very focused on work at those times! And, of course, the lunch hour is a bad time to phone unless you just want to leave a message. Generally, if you want someone to get information for you, a mid-week call might get a result by Friday. A reminder on Thursday afternoon doesn't hurt, as it then becomes an urgent task for them to do by the end of the week!'

How should I handle incoming telephone calls?

In some jobs, like in a sales department, press office, or doctor's reception, handling incoming telephone calls is a major part of the day. How you handle callers will give an immediate impression about you and your company so it's well worth practising and getting right. If you are capable of taking calls efficiently you will save your time and the caller's time, and will give a good impression.

❑ Always have a notepad and pen next to your phone.

❑ Answer promptly – within five rings.

❑ Say a greeting, your name and department or company and ask for a response. This lets the caller get used to the sound of your voice, and know if he or she has reached the right person. ('Good morning, Alma Geddon, Imperial Fireworks, how can I help?')

❑ Identify the caller. ('Who am I speaking to?')

❑ Listen carefully and take notes – such as the caller's name and telephone number and their request. Always write down the name first, and use it again in the conversation to show you have been paying attention.

❑ Indicate you understand by repeating their words or summarising.

❑ Speak clearly and concisely.

❑ Make sure the caller knows what actions you will take.)'Mr Lucifer, I will call you back with the prices for 3,000 Mega-bomb Starburst rockets by the end of the week.')

❑ Don't keep the caller on hold for ages while you try to find out more information or the right person to contact. Take a message if you can't immediately give them the information.

❑ If you can't handle the query, make sure the caller understands how it will be dealt with.

Voicemail and messages

Many companies have voicemail or message systems with a customised greeting on their phone. Make sure your message is clear and concise, and gives callers the opportunity to try another number to speak to a real person. If you leave a time or day on your message, make sure you update it regularly.

Phone calls should be returned as quickly as possible – so make sure you check your voicemail frequently, and note down the caller's details. When you have been away from your desk for a while, give yourself 10 or 20 minutes to listen to all your voicemail and return the calls.

How do I deal with the in-tray and paperwork?

> 'The historian essentially wants more documents than he can really use; the dramatist only wants more liberties than he can really take.'
> Jerome James, *The Aspern Papers*

The paperless office does not exist. Technology, rather than reducing the number of trees used has a multiplier effect – particularly photocopiers. For safety most of us act as historians, keeping endless archives 'just in case'.

To keep the beast under control requires ruthless self-discipline. You need to:

❑ Only keep essential documents, and have a systematic method of storage.

❑ File things in the wastepaper (or recycling) bin as often as you can.

❑ Touch each document only once if possible – if you've read it and dealt with it, you don't need to pick it up again.

❑ Stop unnecessary paper from getting to you in the first place.

❑ Take notes from meetings and telephone calls in an organised way, not on scraps of paper that get invariably get lost.

Your existing papers can be sorted into:

1. File – store for reference or future attention.

2. Action – work needed now.

3. Pass on – someone else should deal with.

4. The bin – no value.

The in-tray

The types of documents that land in your in-tray will be letters in the morning post, company memos at any time during the day, and telephone messages if you have been away from your desk. Don't let the in-tray build up over days or weeks with unlooked-at correspondence – it will only get harder to face.

When you get a new document scan it and store it in the right place immediately. Don't put it back in the in-tray to think about. If it's that vague, it probably belongs in the bin.

Sort your in-tray by A B C – Action now, Begin action, Consider action:

A Immediate action can be taken – do it now. (For example, a message requesting that you send the company brochure.)

B Action can be started but not completed. Put in pending files of ongoing work or a bring-forward system, and make a note on the action list. (For example, a memo from accounts giving figures for a report you are writing.)

C Items for information or reading. If it is short read it quickly. If it is longer put it in a separate file to consume in a time set aside for reading. (For example, a press clipping of one of your company's new products.)

If it's irrelevant throw it away immediately. (For example, a sales offer for a product you wouldn't buy.)

The short-gap file for unproductive time

In order to use those gaps in the day which seem non-productive –
when you are waiting for a meeting to start, travelling, or waiting for a
phone call; have a folder with you with 'small' tasks in it – the report to
proof, list of memos to write, or article to read. (Don't carry around the
whole magazine – tear out or copy the pieces you want.)

Filing

You have to be able to find papers and documents quickly. This applies
to work in progress and reference files.

For reference material group files by broad subject category – eg
Administration, Projects, Training, and then organise them in
alphabetical order. Within each file, arrange the contents in reverse
chronological order – with the most recent document at the top.

Store the current project files you are working on close to your desk –
ideally in the desk drawer – but keep the number to the minimum.
Move them to your reference system if they are not active.

You will have material that must be dealt with at some point in the
future, but that you are not actually working on this week. A 'bring-
forward' system helps deal with this, linked to the reminders you have
already noted in your diary.

A simple folder containing material in date order can suffice.
Alternatively organise 12 files, one for each month of the year. Put each
paper in the relevant month for action when you receive it. This month's
folder becomes your action file. At the beginning of each month pick up
the relevant folder and sort it by date and priority. You may need to
break it down into weeks, and every Monday morning you could check
to see what your priorities are that week.

How do I read effectively?

Not every document you receive has to be studied word for word. Before you start ploughing through pages of text, decide how you will read it:

1. Scan, to see what it is about.
2. Skim or digest reading to get a general overview.
3. Speed reading – to consume quickly.
4. Detailed study – reading carefully to understand in depth.

For example, there is no point in reading a newsletter in detail if it's not relevant to you, and why skim a training course schedule when you know you will have to study the contents to get the benefits?

Scanning
Look at the headings and any bullet points only – is there anything relevant to you?

Digest reading
For books and long reports read the contents list (so you know what it covers), the introduction and conclusion. Read the introduction and last pages of relevant chapters (which should give a summary and any conclusions reached), and then skim read the chapters quickly.

For articles, read the introduction or précis at the start, and the conclusion. Only go back and read the full article if it seems relevant and you have the time. Train yourself to skim the text quickly, not reading every word. If a section or paragraph is particularly interesting, re-read it more slowly.

Speed reading
To speed read effectively you will need to spend time practising the skills, and it may not be that appropriate to your job. Speed reading means training your eyes not to move along lines of text from left to right, but to move vertically down the page, recognising the sense of groups of words.

26

Study reading

If you have a complex document that requires concentration to understand, make sure you have a block of time available, in a quiet place where you won't be interrupted.

Take notes and use highlighters or pens to identify the important points. (Take a copy first, if it's a document you shouldn't be writing on.) If you have a question, write it down immediately next to the text – so you don't have to remember where or what it was later.

How do I deal with email?

Email is increasingly taking the place of letters and memos because it is very easy to use, and many companies now have networks and computer facilities for most members of staff. In fact, email is too easy, so it is not unusual for people to have several dozen messages a day, many of which are irrelevant.

To save time with your email, learn efficient habits. You should:

❑ Put aside a set time in the day to look at your in-tray – don't dip in and out several times, or stop what you're doing every time the computer pings with a new message.

❑ Organise your computer folders so emails that need to be stored are kept together by subject. Just like paper documents, you should throw away the ones you don't need to keep for reference.

❑ Read and respond to messages immediately – don't leave them to come back to if you can help it.

❑ If you can tell from the headline it's junk or not relevant to you, don't bother to spend time reading it – just dump it.

❑ Avoid printing email messages unless they are reference documents and need to go into files or be discussed at meetings.

When sending email (especially to anyone outside your own company) get into the habit of using it as a proper business communication tool:

❏ Always put an appropriate title in the subject field – so the reader knows what it is about.

❏ Use language effectively, with good English and correct spelling. Always be polite and concise in email.

❏ Don't send large attachments, but if you can't avoid doing so, make sure the person receiving it has a version of software that can read it. (Unless you want to spend the afternoon on the phone discussing technical issues with someone who would prefer to receive your document than your computing advice.)

❏ Choose who is copied on the message carefully. Don't send it to people who don't need it – like you they'll just dump it, and get irritated by the waste of time.

Whatever you do, don't send an email to avoid speaking to someone. If the message is delicate, personal or urgent, or if a conversation is needed to negotiate the matter, then a phone call is more appropriate. It will probably be quicker, too.

How do I use technology effectively?

Technology is fun, and can really speed up work processes. It can also be a huge time waster, and extremely frustrating, if you can't get it working properly. If you are using complicated equipment and software:

❏ Make sure you know how to get help if things go wrong.
❏ Invest in training time.

The personal computer

Computers and software programmes are increasing in their complexity and sophistication continually. If a PC is to work as a power tool for you then you need to spend time practising using it, and looking after it.

1. Organise your PC – invest time in good file management. Store your documents in subject folders and name them appropriately so you can find them easily. (Some companies have guidelines on file naming and file management – if so, make sure you follow them.)

2. Make sure your PC has all the software you need on it to do your job. But watch out for the things that cause wasted time and frustration. For instance, always virus check disks that come to you from any other computer. Don't load software that looks fun and just creates hassle for you or your computer support staff when it interferes with other programs. If you can't resist playing them, remove any games packages from your computer. They're not appropriate in the office and are big time wasters.

3. Find out about training courses to increase your competence and confidence. Get hold of manuals for help with using the functions of your software more efficiently.

4. Make sure there is a back-up procedure in place for the data on your computer, or copy important documents to disk regularly. Save your document every ten minutes as you work – you can waste a lot of time redoing work that's lost if your computer crashes.

5. Send faxes straight from your computer if you can – rather than printing and faxing separately.

6. If your company provides it, use an electronic diary like Microsoft Scheduler or Lotus Organiser. They contain many advanced features, including alarm clocks to remind you of meetings.

Top time tip – learn to walk away from your computer

Guy Dance looks after the computer lab in a school. Everyone comes to him with their computer problems and tasks, including the school admin staff. He has two important tips for staff and students. 'First, if you start to get frustrated, something's going wrong, and you are just spending time getting worked up – stand up and walk away. Go and do something else for 30 minutes, and if you can't sort the problem when you're calm, get help. If you've got to wait for help, wait.'

'Second, don't waste time waiting for the computer to finish doing things – it's clever and it's fast, but it can't do everything at once. If you send a big document to print, it'll tie up the computer for a while. Send it at 12.25 and go out to lunch. Don't send it at 9.30am and have nothing to do for half an hour.'

Personal organisers

Personal organisers – or personal digital assistants – are mini-pocket sized computers. The simple ones combine electronic diaries and address books.

There are many more sophisticated organisers now available, which have advanced software to write notes, send email or work on spreadsheets, and can be connected to a desktop computer to transfer diary information and other data.

If you can invest the time in learning how to use the organiser – and you are good at typing – then they are very helpful. (Some now have handwriting recognition, so typing isn't necessary.) Otherwise stick to a diary or filofax, which can be much quicker!

Dictaphones and tape recorders

Originally dictaphones were used to record memos and letters for secretaries to type up. They can be useful tools for people who travel a great deal. Recording points or ideas in one place as they occur is often quicker and more fluid than writing down notes.

Top time tip – don't rely on your memory to record everything

Ed Liner is a journalist on a local paper. He works freelance and has an office and computer at home. His dictaphone is a great labour-saving tool. 'I often come across stories when I'm out during the day, or have a bright idea or a new lead to follow. I used to keep a notebook, but it was always going missing when I needed it for an important entry, and then I'd have forgotten later. If I did get stories down in it, I'd have to transcribe them on to my computer later. Now I carry a dictaphone wherever I go, to collect thoughts, ideas, and interviews with people. I can just play it back at home and type up what I need. It saves a lot of time – and rescues many good stories from dissolving into the ether!'

What are the golden rules of personal time management?

'The miracles that have been held up to us in praise of work are a little unfortunate. "How doth the little busy bee improve each shining hour, and gather honey all the day from every opening flower." Well he does not. He spends most of the day in buzzing and aimless aerobatics, and gets about a fifth of the honey he would collect if he organised himself.'

Sir Heneage Oglivie

Spend time organising and planning

Set up a fixed daily routine with times for everyday matters like dealing with correspondence, telephone calls and discussions with colleagues. Spend time each day reviewing the action list and diary and setting time aside for specific tasks.

Analyse your minute burglars

Diagnose the interruptions or habits that are stealing your time, and do something about them. Be aware constantly of what you are doing – is it the best use of time right now?

Finish things

Set deadlines for yourself on small tasks and complete them so they aren't around to be bothersome. Do things well enough, without being overly perfectionist.

Prepare, and do things once

When dealing with any task or problem – get the preparation done so you can get it right first time and don't have to start, stop and start again or re-do work.

Don't procrastinate

Putting off the difficult and unpleasant doesn't make it go away. It will usually stay in your subconscious weighing it down, and making you less able to concentrate on other things.

Combine tasks when you can

If you need to speak to someone about four different things – have them all ready for a single conversation, don't call up several times.

McCormack

31

Use every minute you can
Pockets of waiting or 'dead' time are inevitable – have a file handy of short-gap fillers so you can read or think rather than becoming impatient with the waste of time.

Book time for heavy thinking
If you have work to do that requires concentration – book time for it and find a place to work where you won't be interrupted.

Be selective
Choose to do the important tasks, and learn to say no to the ones that are not important.

Manage information
Deal with information overload by learning to sift the material you get and read it effectively.

Relax too
Allow time in the day for relaxation – make sure you take a lunch break, because brains need rest. Arrange breaks for times when you can't work effectively.

Don't take work home
Unless you are positive you will do something about it, it's better to separate work and leisure.

Top time tip – don't carry your desk home
Prue Frieder is an editor in a publishing company. She spends a lot of her day liaising with other departments, authors, printers and freelancers. She has lots of reading too – manuscripts, reports, book catalogues. 'I spent so much time during the day on the telephone and doing admin, I began to think that it was easier to take the reading work home to do quietly in the evenings and weekends. Big mistake. All you do is put things off and then tip the contents of your desk into your briefcase, go home and spend the evening not knowing where to start, feeling guilty about not doing it, and lugging it back in the next day. Now I make sure I have time at the office to get my work done, and if I really need to take something home, the rule is to take *one task only*, which can be done in half an hour. I start it, I finish it, and I don't break my arms carting the office about.'

4. How do I practise good time management when working with others?

Time management would be terribly easy – if other people weren't involved! How you handle interruptions, communications, meetings and emergencies will really impact on the time you have available to do things.

How do I work with others to avoid interruptions?

There is a very fine balancing act necessary when you work with other people. You have to gauge the amount of time you spend getting to know them in order to communicate well, without letting the social side of your workplace take over from the jobs that need to be done.

The best technique is to be straightforward.

'Juliet, I'd really like to hear about your honeymoon but I have a deadline to meet. Can you give me those sales figures, and let's have lunch together tomorrow for a good chat.'

'Norman, I'm concentrating on finishing a report at the moment. Could we get together later at 4pm to discuss the office layout?'

If you have the luxury of a private office you can establish 'red' and 'green' time by closing the door when you don't want to be interrupted or leaving it open when you are available. Some time management courses suggest that even in an open plan office you can set up a 'do not disturb' sign on your desk – you will have to find out whether this is acceptable in the culture of your own company, and make sure others agree to it. Unless something is a real emergency most people respect your priorities – providing another time is arranged to deal with their issues.

Equally, you need to be able to approach other people for help. If you show that you respect they have other things to do, they will be more inclined to help you as quickly as they can. Here are some simple rules for managing your time around others.

❏ Always give advance warning.

❏ Try to avoid asking someone to do something urgently – and don't stand over their desk while they do it. (Go away and do something in your short-gap folder.)

❏ Make it clear exactly what help you need, and how long it will take.

❏ If it involves a meeting or training session, let the other person choose a convenient time for them.

Top time tip – others can't react instantly

Justin Door is an executive officer with the Civil Service. His advice is: 'If you have loads of different tasks to do in one day, any that involve other people should come first. You need to give them time to give their input, which may be as simple as a signature on a letter, to reading a long document that is to go to another government department. So whether it's my boss or a colleague, I approach people in the morning if I need their reaction or time by the end of the day – they can fit the task in for when it's most convenient. Also they're more likely to do it quickly or efficiently, as they don't feel pressured by it, because I never ask them to do it that instant.'

How do I manage the boss?

Your supervisor will have the most influence on how you spend your time. Their job is to set your priorities and targets for the company's benefit, and help you meet them.

Managers have an unfortunate habit of asking people to do things they might not really want to do themselves, and thinking that their view on priorities is more important than anyone else's.

There are three options:

1. Ignore your boss, and expect to change job involuntarily.
2. Do what you are told, however much you disagree.
3. Learn to reach a joint agreement.

To illustrate, you are concentrating on finishing a proposal for an important client when your boss walks over to your desk and says, 'Can you get last month's sales figures together for me?'

Do you say, 'No. I'm busy right now, go bother someone else.'

Or, 'Alllllllrrright', heave and sigh, closing your files as loudly as possible, realising you will probably have to work late and making it very clear to everyone around you that you're not happy about it.

Or, 'How urgently do you need them, because I'm trying to finish this proposal to Smith & Co – could anyone else do it?'

It is probably not a good idea to abruptly say 'No' to your more senior colleagues. Managing your boss, so that you can plan your own time, is about communication. Make sure you know his or her view on priorities (they may be set by someone more senior). Make sure that your own plans, workload and long-term objectives are understood.

How do I manage myself if I'm my own boss?

Many people work on their own, either setting up their own company or selling a skill to individual clients. Some examples would be a gardener, freelance consultant, writer, window cleaner, designer, accountant.

All the golden rules of time management apply to people who work independently – in fact, it is especially important that their time is well spent. Very often they are paid on an hourly rate, or given a project fee based on the time the job should take and the materials needed. This means that time spent travelling to see clients, eating lunch, going to the bank etc, is time that is not earning money.

If you work from home, you don't have the problem of interruptions from colleagues, but it is more than likely your friends and family will interrupt you! It is easy to assume that someone at home is always available for telephone chats or a coffee break.

If you live with other people, there may be expectations that you will take on more domestic responsibilities during the day – cleaning, shopping, washing – and these are distractions that will eat into your time.

Here are some suggestions for people who work on their own:

❑ Schedule your day for work and routine breaks – say 'no' to unscheduled breaks suggested by friends or neighbours popping in, or agree times when you are available.

❑ Arrange meetings or appointments in clusters, or at least on the same day, so your travel time is reduced.

❑ Don't let domestic tasks like grocery shopping or collecting the dry cleaning dominate the day – fit it in around journeys to meetings.

❑ Set aside a few hours a week to do any administration you have – such as your bookkeeping. Put it in your diary and stick to it. Don't leave your accounts to build up over months or it will be a frightening task to face!

❏ Better still, find someone else to do your admin. Don't attempt to be your own bookkeeper, secretary or plumber just because you work from home – you're not earning money when you're doing 'nonchargeable' tasks.

❏ Time all your work and keep a note of it so you know exactly how long each job takes. This will help for scheduling future work (and negotiating realistic fees).

❏ Stick to the 'don't take work home' principle! Set the tasks you want to complete each day and a time for finishing. It's not efficient – or healthy – to work through the night, or constantly take on jobs with tight deadlines so you forget what the weekends are for.

Top time tip – if a job's worth doing, it's worth preparing well

Ricky Tee is a carpenter who specialises in making customised shelving and cupboards in people's homes. When he is briefed about a job, he has to give a quote which includes the wood and other materials used, and the likely time it will take him. He has to keep to the time he quotes as his clients are eager for him to get finished and get out of their house!

Ricky says, 'The key to finishing a job on time is starting it well prepared. I know exactly what I am going to be doing, and I make sure I have all the materials with me – down to the last nail – as well as checking that all my tools are in order. If in the middle of a job you suddenly have to go out to the shops because you've run out of rawl plugs, you could lose an hour in the day – an hour you can't spare when the client is coming home at 5.30pm and expects the job done. I check my toolbox regularly and I never go out to a job without a good supply of standard equipment.'

How do I say no?

There are good reasons to turn down requests – for instance, you don't know how to do something, you have a heavy workload already, it's not part of your work or priorities, or it would be more appropriate for someone else to do it.

Most people find it hard to say no. It makes them feel bad, mean and unhelpful – colleagues won't like them. But saying no, in the right way for the right reasons, will save you time. It will stop you doing unimportant things to please people, and it will allow you to focus on doing your own tasks well. Agreeing to do everything can be a real stress creator because of the worry of trying to fit everything in and the potential guilt of letting others down. It is much better to tell a colleague that you won't be able to help them by doing a piece of work, than to say you will do it, and then not be able to.

Choosing when and how to say no is a skill successful people master.

When is it appropriate to say no?

❏ If you have other commitments.

❏ If the request is outside your responsibilities.

❏ If saying yes will impact on the success of other work.

How do you say no?

You must be firm without being rude or aggressive. Say the word no first, but then add an apology or explanation to be polite.

> 'No, I can't make your meeting at 5pm, I've got to finish a report.'
>
> 'No, I'm sorry I won't be able to help with the charity collections this month.'
>
> 'No, I can't come round to talk about new computer systems this morning, but I have some free time tomorrow.'

By remaining calm, and speaking steadily, you can avoid appearing aggressive or causing upset. Most people will accept a logical and firm refusal. For the more persistent you may have to repeat yourself, but do so patiently.

How do I make sure meetings are a good use of time?

Why hold a meeting? If you have a task or project to complete which needs input from several people then a meeting is the best way of progressing work.

Start by deciding whether the meeting is really necessary. Could the business be discussed by phone, or information communicated in a letter or report? Calculate the cost of the meeting in people time, the time spent organising plus the travel time and meeting time for all attendees multiplied by their hourly rate. Meetings can be very expensive!

Consider running a telephone conference or video conference if people are a long way away and an interactive conversation is absolutely essential.

The big time wasters in meetings are delayed starts, unprepared participants (who don't have the right information and need briefing) and display equipment that doesn't work properly. You can avoid all of these problems with good preparation.

If you want an in-house company meeting to be brief, don't provide chairs and don't provide refreshments.

If you are chairing the meeting, decide on the precise objectives and communicate them to all participants. Make sure the right people are invited and they know what preparation they will need to do before the meeting starts. Prepare a logical agenda of the subjects to be covered.

Start the meeting on time with introductions and a prepared statement of the objectives and goals. Encourage participation but don't allow the discussion to drift to other topics.

Summarise the agreed points and record decisions, actions to be taken and who is responsible for them.

How do I handle emergencies?

Unexpected events and emergencies do occur from time to time. In a crisis the elapsed time before you start solving the problem should be as small as possible. It's terribly easy to get sucked into the excitement of a sudden drama – where everyone stops work to talk about it or panic, and nothing actually happens to deal with it.

Emergencies can vary from issues like spotting an error in a brochure that has just gone to press (which may cost a lot of money to put right, even if there's time), to the canteen flooding and everyone in the building being evacuated.

For physical emergencies, there will be formal office health and safety procedures to follow. Make sure you know about these and behave appropriately so you can help others to control or contain the problem. You may be the fire monitor or health and safety officer for your floor and will know exactly what to do – do it immediately, or do as you are told by the relevant person – quickly and calmly.

Hopefully you won't face any really serious disaster in your workplace. But from time to time other types of emergency will occur – such as salvaging an expensive print-run, or having to spend a week doing urgent work for a colleague who is suddenly taken ill. Don't panic. Keep your head:

❑ Respond quickly – but don't over dramatise.

❑ Admit any faults that might have contributed to the problem and ask for help from the right people.

❑ Explain what is happening to anyone who needs to know (not everyone who looks interested).

❑ Decide who should deal with the problem.

❑ Watch out for people taking advantage of the crisis to waste time or jump on the excitement bandwagon.

❑ Look at your diary and action list – see what needs to be re-prioritised.

Formal disaster recovery or emergency plans are often prepared by big companies, and practised by the staff. For instance, British Airways has a well-rehearsed plan for handling press and enquiries should any of their aeroplanes get into difficulties.

The company can decide in advance:

❏ What work can be delayed.

❏ What work must be continued and who should deal with it.

❏ Who will undertake specific actions.

❏ What communications need to be sent and to whom.

❏ A list of emergency numbers.

'Crisis? I thought this was normal.'

Remember that crisis management is about dealing with a genuine crisis. It shouldn't be the standard working practice. Learn to manage your time, and you will avoid turning your every working day into a panic of urgent tasks, missed deadlines and lost opportunities.

5. Where can I find out more?

Who could I contact?

British Psychological Society
48 Princess Road East, Leicester LE1 7DR
Tel: 0116 254 9568

Filofax UK
Unit 3, Victoria Gardens
Burgess Hill, West Sussex RH15 9NB
Tel: 01444 238100

The Industrial Society
Information Services
Robert Hyde House, 48 Bryanston Square
London W1H 7LN
Tel: 0171 479 2000

Institute of Management
3rd Floor, 2 Savoy Court
Strand, London WC2R 0EZ
Tel: 0171 497 0580

Institute of Personnel and Development
IPD House
35 Camp Road, Wimbledon
London SW19 4UX
Tel: 0181 971 9000

Time Manager International
50 High Street
Henley in Arden
Solihull , West Midlands B95 5AN
Tel: 01564 794100

What publications could I look at?

Time management is an important skill whatever type of work you do,
and there are many sources of good advice. The following is a selection
of resources available.

*Executive time management: Getting 12 hours work out of an 8-hour
    day,* Helen Reynolds and Mary E Tramel, Gower 1996
First things first, Stephen R Covey, Simon & Schuster 1994
How to use Microsoft Outlook, Deborah Lewites, Ziff Davis 1997
*If you haven't got the time to do it right, when will you find the time to
    do it over?* Jeffrey J Mayer, Fireside 1990
Manage your time, Iain Maitland, Institute of Personnel and
    Development 1995
Managing your time – 3 video cassettes, BBC
Slowing down to the speed of life, Richard Carson and Joseph Bailey,
    Hodder & Stoughton 1998
Teach yourself time management, Polly Bird, Hodder & Stoughton
    1998
The complete idiot's guide to managing your time, Jeff Davidson, Alpha
    1995
The organised executive: 101 ways to manage time, people and paper,
    Stephanie Winston, Kogan Page 1994
The seven habits of highly effective people, Stephen R Covey, Simon &
    Schuster 1992

After finishing university, you should be smart enough to spot a good deal when you see one.

As a graduate, we can offer you a first class package including:

- Special offers on graduate overdrafts and loans.
- Primeline, our 24 hour person-to-person telephone banking service.
- Commission-free travellers cheques and currency.
- And many other benefits.

If you'd like more details, simply call us on the number below.

0800 200 400
Monday-Friday 8am-8pm, Saturday 9am-6pm
www.natwest.co.uk

NatWest
More than just a bank